úr Njáls sögu:

„með lögum skal land byggja"

from the Nials Saga:

„with laws the country should be built up"

Understanding - Tolerance - Realisation

Carl Joh. Jac. Keyser

About the Icelandic Republic and its decline

Translated from the Swedish original, with illustrations and a detailed glossary,

and published

by **Albert George Viktorsson Trolle**

Iarnwith in the year 2023

Imprint

Bibliographic information of the German National Library:

The German National Library lists this publication in the German National Bibliography; detailed bibliographic data are available on the Internet at http://dnb.dnb.de.

Copy editing: alphagam

Production and publishing house: BoD – Books on Demand, Norderstedt

ISBN: 9783757845612

TIGER

AF TRAWENDAHL

Foreword.

When "Janne" Keyser wrote his treatise, as he himself called it, on the Icelandic Republic and its decline in 1848, a revolution was raging on the continent in the small German states in order to achieve what the Icelanders had already achieved in 930, namely a national assembly.

But Keyser also describes how the privilege of a people (in those days only men of fighting age) deciding their own destiny was once again given away.

It was all about vanity, greed for power and the concentration of wealth. When each individual thinks only of himself, even the most progressive social order disintegrates. And that is why the failure of the Icelandic Republic is still so relevant today. When individuals take advantage of a system for their own benefit, it becomes dangerous for everyone...

"Democracy arises when one strives for freedom and equality of all citizens and takes into account the number of citizens, but not their specific nature."

Aristoteles (384 until 322 BC), Greek universal scholar

In the translation I have tried to follow the original text closely. But I have also tried to put it into words that can be understood today. Another aim was to preserve something of the ancient language and its character, and thus make the thoughts of the ancients visible.

For a better understanding, and because some of the words and events are not so familiar to us today, I have included an extensive glossary.

This work is dedicated to my family and especially to my wife for her endless patience and understanding.

Albert George Viktorsson Trolle,

Iarnwith in Juli 2023

About the Icelandic Republic
and its decline.

Just as Ingiald Illråda[A] burned Uppsala in order to break the power of the fylke kings and make himself and his successors the sole kings of the entire Svear kingdom, so Harald Hårfager[B] about a century later worked to establish his sole rule in Norway, finally breaking the rule of the petty kings with the victory at Hafursfjord. It should come as no surprise that the change in circumstances displeased many, especially those who felt humiliated by it. Both those who hated the king as an overwhelming victor and those who saw him as a high-handed autocrat immediately seized every opportunity to escape his oppressive sceptre. One such opportunity was the recent discovery of Iceland. This island was now to be the refuge of those who had been deprived of their freedom and rights at home. Discovered around 860 by Gardar Svafarsson[C], it was later visited during a passing voyage by Naddod and finally (in 868) by Floke, who had purposefully set out on this voyage. However, as he did not feel comfortable there in view of the harsh climate (which is why he also called the island Iceland), he returned to Norway after some time. The existence of Iceland was now, after so many visits there, beyond any doubt; but it did not acquire permanent inhabitants until 874, when two Norwegians, Ingolf and Leif[D], made their second journey to it and settled there.

The reason for their journey and emigration was due to individual circumstances. They were the grandchildren of murderers, had committed manslaughter themselves and, as outlaws, were forced to leave their homeland. That outlaws were not absent from the great exodus between 874 and 934, the extent of which is attested to by Are Frode[E] when he tells us that the Wise Men said that Iceland would be full after 60 winters, as it had never been before[1], is quite probable. However, it is a great mistake to assume that the majority of these emigrants were adventurers and outlaws, for it is certain that they came from the most distinguished families in Norway and were those who possessed sufficient wealth to equip themselves for such a long journey in search of peace, comfort and independence in faraway Iceland.

--- This is also confirmed by Geijer[F] when he says: "Various circumstances made Iceland a desirable place of refuge." He added: "Many gave up their fatherland rather than submit to his (Harald Hårfager's) yoke, and great emigrations took place from Norway."[2] The excellent Danish historian Peterson also agrees in this respect when he writes: "The immediate cause of the emigration was given by the conquests of Harald Haarfager in Norway; he forced the most respectable men to submit or go into exile, seized all the land property, even the lakes and forests, and made all the peasants his liegemen."

"This was outrageous to many rich and powerful Norsemen; they retreated to the Faroe Islands, the archipelago and other islands in the West Sea, from where they plundered the coasts of Norway in the summer and usually retreated to Iceland"[3].

As for the nature of this island, which became a new Scandinavian settlement, for the Swedes and Danes also found their way to these remote shores[4], the first explorers, as we have already mentioned, gave very different descriptions.

Of these, the closest to the truth was the one that described Iceland as a country whose surface was mostly covered with snow and ice, but in whose interior a fierce volcanic fire raged, which from time to time broke through the ice and snow and flooded the surrounding districts with rock and water --- as a country in which there were valleys where, protected from the cold of the sea by large forests, grass could grow and grain (though not sufficient for the needs of the country) could be grown and harvested --- as a land, finally, that was certainly suitable for livestock and fishing, as the cattle could feed themselves in winter, the waters were rich in salmon and all kinds of fish, and the coasts were favourable for whaling.
This is a brief description of the nature of Iceland at the time when the Scandinavian emigrants took possession of it.

For the seizure itself and the events observed during it, we think it best to refer to Petersen and Geijer[5]. What followed was the emergence of the Härad[G].

This arose around the leader, who, having divided among his companions the ground previously consecrated, continued to be, as during the voyage, so now on land, the first man among his own. As such he was high priest and judge at the Thing, and was therefore called Godordman, or orator in the name of the gods, and the oldest designation for such an area was Godord[H]. As such he also made laws together with his circle [of followers], which as a whole was distinct and separate from other circles as a small whole for themselves.

--- In this way, a series of small communities emerged which were isolated from each other and had no connection with each other[6]. It was natural that under such conditions situations arose in which questions of public interest were raised by which the need for a link uniting all these individual links into a coherent chain was recognised and such a link was missed. It was no less natural that between the chiefs themselves, as the defenders of their own circles [/ followings, ed.], quarrels arose from the desire of one to encroach upon or interfere with the rights of his neighbour, or from the fact that one saw himself at a disadvantage through the rights of the other.

Moreover, as there was no common law, there was no obstacle to these courtiers permitting themselves any wrong against each other. All this, the one with the other, made that it was seen to be necessary and useful, at the suggestion of the old and wise UlfliotI, to establish a general assembly and supreme court common to all the Godords of the land, to be held annually, and called the Althing[J]. --- This was done in the year 928. --- This Althing was to be the supreme court to which cases should be referred from places of jurisdiction of the Godords for final decision; and in this respect it was a superior court [court of appeal]. Moreover, general matters were to be discussed and decided there, and laws for the whole country were to be passed and publicly announced there with the consent of the whole people; and in this respect the Althing was a common general assembly. --- The chairman was the "Lagman"[K]. He was the highest secular official on the island, and his office at first lasted as long as his lifetime. Later the office was reduced to a "comfortable" period, i.e. it lasted as long as the chiefs and the people were satisfied with him. Three years, however, seems to have been the usual term of office[7]. --- Thus the separate parts of Iceland had been united into a whole; but the measures and steps taken were not sufficient to produce fully the effects they intended. Still remained the many chiefs of equal dignity, but of differing strength and spirit, now no more bound by the law than before. Nothing was more natural, therefore, than that all quarrels among themselves should continue as long as the rights of the weaker were not secured against the encroachments of the stronger.

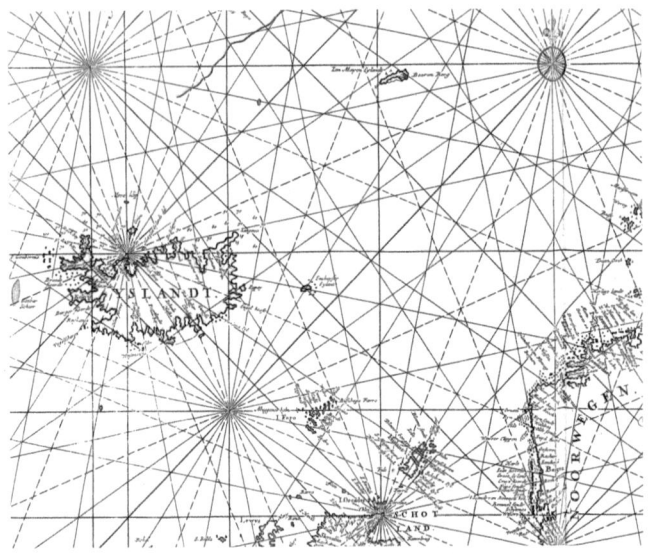

Extract from: Keulen, Johannes van, „De Zee Custen van Noorwegen, Finmarcken, Laplant, Ruslant, Spitzbergen en Yslandt", Amsterdam 1681; Det Kgl. Bibliotek, kbk_2_45_01_028, 2021-10-12

Iceland, thus torn apart by internal disagreements and conflicts, was meanwhile the object of Norway's incessant lustful gaze. Attempts at unification were not disregarded either, albeit with varying degrees of success. For this reason, too, Olof Tryggvason[L] resorted to a means which might have been successful had he left the execution of his plan to wiser and less wild and impetuous men. The object of this king's intentions in Iceland was indeed to soften the mind there by the introduction of Christianity, to bring the whole island into closer contact with the mother country, and finally to restore it to his dominion, and thereby both to deprive the rebellious subjects of a suitable and safe refuge from his punishing arm, and to free the coasts of Norway from the annual depredations caused no less by necessity than by lust. --- That here, as in piety and Christianity, is to be sought the true cause of the eagerness and perseverance with which he undertook and carried out this cause, is probably beyond all doubt. --- --- Now, there had always been a communion between Iceland and Norway, the reason for which was to be found in the inability of the former to form an isolated state because of the scarcity of nature and the severity of the climate; but to make this communion firmer, to secure its continuance, was what Olof Tryggvason wished to effect by the introduction of Christianity. - To this end he sent Stefner Thorgilson[M] in 996. The reason for the failure of this first attempt may have been both the sharp-sightedness of the Icelanders, who saw through Olof's plan, and Stefner's violent action, which eventually also forced him to return[8]. Undeterred by such a beginning, however, King Olof sent a new apostle to Iceland the very next year (997). This was Thangbrand[N], of whom it is said in history that he was a great fighter, but at the same time a good writer and a steadfast man[9]. But he too did little, or at least not nearly as much as he could have done had he not added to his other qualities that of a great fighter[10]. Finally (1000), after two failed attempts, Olof succeeded in having Christianity accepted at the Althing by two Icelanders baptised by Thangbrand, Gissur the White[O] and Hjalte Skeggeson[11].

We felt that the clearest and most vivid picture of the Icelanders' way of life and their interaction with each other would be found in the stories of two outstanding men who are so closely linked that one cannot be told without telling most of the other. - We are referring to the stories of Gunnar and Nial[P]. The main reason for quoting from the latter is to provide information about the origin of the Femtardom, the Court of Five. We now turn to an account of some events from these stories, and have followed the account given by Petersen in his work (Danmarks Historie i Hedenold[12]) and often quoted by us.

Gunnar Hamundson, who came from Baug, lived at Hlidarende in Fliothshlid[Q]; his brother's name was Kolskägg. Gunnar was a tall and strong man who could hack and throw spears with both hands. He swung his sword so that it appeared to be tripled in the air; he swam like a seal and was the best archer in the land. As a relative and friend of Unna (Rut's wife, a grandson of Thorsten Röde) he was asked by her to claim her marriage rights from Rut. Gunnar said that this was a rather difficult matter and asked her to bear in mind that her father, who was a man of the law, could do nothing, and he, who knew little about such matters, had even less chance of success. In the meantime, he decided to turn to Nial, the most knowledgeable man of law in the land, who lived in Bergthorshvol[R] at the time. Nial was the man to turn to when people were in distress, and he helped everyone as long as it was not against the law. Although Nial found the matter rather difficult and told Gunnar so, he promised to give him the best advice he could. Then, after being silent for a while, he said: "I have thought it over and it will be all right; you shall ride out from home tomorrow with two others. Over your good clothes you shall put on a coarse, reddish-brown cloak and a raincoat over it. Each of you shall have two horses, one fat and one lean, and you shall carry with you all kinds of blacksmith's work. When you have crossed the moor, you shall pull your hat down over your ears, and if anyone asks who you are, your companions shall answer that you are the famous Köphedin (Kaupa-Hedinn) from Öfjord, who travels with blacksmith's wares. The latter is a hot-tempered man who thinks he understands everything and lashes out at people who do not do what he wants. Then ride to Borgfjord and sell your wares everywhere, spending time in the process. Then ride to Norderådal, Rutfjord and Laxådal until you reach Höskuldstad. You must spend the night there. The next morning you go to the nearest farm near Rutstad, offer your things, take out the worst and try to hide the defects. But the farmer will examine the goods carefully and find the defect. Then you should get angry and take it away from him, accusing him. He replies that you could not be expected to treat him well, since you are mean to everyone. Then you pounce on him (even if you are not used to it), but be careful not to reveal who you are by using all your strength.

Now messengers will be sent to Rut to ask him to come and separate you. He will come immediately and invite you to join him. You will accept the invitation and sit down on the lower bench directly opposite the High Chair, whichever seat he assigns you. When he asks you if you are from Nordland, answer that you are from Öfjord." --- So Nial went on to answer some questions that Rut would ask, giving Gunnar instructions on how to answer. Eventually, he said, the speech would turn to Mörd, and to Rut's question of whether Gunnar had heard what had happened between them, he would reply: "Yes, he separated you from your wife without you being able to prevent it. If, in the course of the conversation, Rut claimed that Mörd should have sued him, Gunnar should ask how he should have proceeded, and after Rut (who had no suspicions about the person he was talking to) had confirmed the lawsuit, Gunnar should repeat the same. Then he could go his way, because the hardest thing would have been done for him: Rut's complaint in such a way that he heard it himself, and in his rightful home. With that Nial finished his advice and added: "We should go to the Thing in the summer and then we will see what we can do. Everything Nial had predicted came to pass. Everything he had told him to do, Gunnar did, and so Rut was sued. So the matter came before the Althing, and Rut, who had been ordered by Gunnar to defend himself, was finally ordered to fight a duel on the island of Öxerå (Öxara), or else accept Unna's right to marry. The money was then paid, for Gunnar was far superior to Rut.

The year 984[s] was a hard one. Gunnar was suffering from a lack of hay and food. So he rode to Otkel in Kyrkeby and asked him to give him some, but he refused, even though he had the opportunity. This was talked about at Nials, and everyone said it was a disgrace to Otkel. What is there to talk about, Bergthora, Nial's wife, said to her husband? It would be much better if you gave him food and hay, for you have plenty of it. - Nial did so. Gunnar's wife, Halgerde, hardly noticed this kindness and helpfulness, but often spoke of Otkel's refusal. While Gunnar was at the Thing, she sent a thrall[T] [a slave] her husband had bought from Otkel to Kyrkeby to steal cheese and butter and then set fire to the house he had visited. On the way back, having successfully completed the task, he forgot his knife and belt after mending his shoestring. These things were found by a cowardly scoundrel, Skamkel on Hof, a friend of Otkel, who now turned to Mörd Valgardson on Hof in Rangevall (Rangarvalli) for advice. In order to get evidence against Gunnar's wife, the cunning Mörd sent beggars around and had them bring him whatever they begged for. So it was that in Hlidarende they were given a cheese that matched the shape of Otkel's cheese. - Since Gunnar had come home in the meantime and Halgerde had laid out butter and cheese for him - things he knew they didn't have in the house - he immediately guessed what had happened. On that occasion they had a quarrel, so violent that he slapped her across the face. Then he rode to Otkel and offered him a fine. But Skamkel persuaded Otkel to reject the offer by agreeing to seek the advice of Gissur the White and Geir the Good[U]. He also went and returned with the false news that they had confirmed the case against Gunnar. So the matter came before the Althing and on Gunnar's side were Höskuld, Rut and Nial. The latter advised that Gunnar should challenge Gissur the White and Blackbeard Geir the Good to a duel. Gissur then asked who had advised him to challenge Gunnar. Otkel replied: "It was your advice and Geir's. Who lies like that, Gissur asked? Skamkel brought me the news, Otkel continued. The bastard, said Gissur - where is he? He is sick at home, Otkel replied - and so he lay at home during the whole session. Gissur left the judgement to Gunnar himself, and so the matter was settled to Gunnar's honour and advantage.

The following year, while Otkel was riding to a feast for Runolf the Gode at Dal, his horse went off with him. Gunnar, who was calmly sowing his field when his enemy passed him by, was wounded in the ear by his riding spur. When this incident was mentioned at the feast, Skamkel said that if Gunnar had been a simple man, he would have admitted that he had cried. This statement was brought to Gunnar's attention by a shepherd who became very angry. He took his weapons and, together with his brother Blackbeard, killed Otkel and seven other men at Rangå[v] (Ranga) while they were on their way home. Geir the Gode was appointed as the prosecutor for the murder of Otkel and his companions. The matter went to the Althing, but Gunnar rejected it, because among the dead was a Norwegian, and Geir the Gode had made a mistake by charging him with manslaughter, because the Norwegian had no [rightful] accuser in the country. The matter was settled with a fine. Shortly afterwards there was a dispute between Gunnar and the sons of Starkotters on the Threehorn. Gunnar and his brother were ambushed at Knafahole and defended themselves against eighteen men, fourteen of whom fell. Meanwhile, a group of Gunnar's enemies had ambushed themselves at Rangå, including Otkel's son Thorgeir. He was killed by Gunnar and the others fled. Gissur the White became the prosecutor. He demanded that Gunnar be condemned to the forest[13], but through Nial's efforts the matter was left to twelve men to decide. They sentenced Gunnar and Blackbeard to fines and three years' exile abroad. Nial comforted Gunnar, who was unhappy with the outcome, and reminded him of the fame he could achieve abroad. The brothers were immediately given a place on a ship. Their belongings were taken on board. Farewells were said in Bergthorshvol and to other friends and acquaintances. Gunnar was already on his way down to the beach to board the ship. But when he looked back at his farm, his fields and meadows, everything seemed so extraordinarily beautiful and subdued at that moment that it seemed impossible to live apart from it. So he decided to stay at home. Blackbeard begged and pleaded with him in vain not to give this pleasure to his enemies. - In the end, he had to travel alone (992). In the meantime, Gunnar was an outlaw and was proclaimed as such by Gissur at the Althing the following summer. At the same time his enemies decided on his death. It was not long before they gathered and set out for Hlidarende. They forced the nearest farmer to lure Gunnar's dog Sam from the farm and killed him. Gunnar, awakened by the howls of death, immediately suspected disaster and said: "You have been tricked, poor Sam, my faithful servant, and the time between your death and mine will probably be short. And so it was.

His enemies attacked the house, and Gunnar defended himself bravely, beating them back three times until one ran forward and cut his bowstring. Then he called to Halgerde: Give me two locks of your hair, and you and my mother will weave me a bowstring! Is this important to you? asked Halgerde. It concerns my life, Gunnar replied. Then let me remind you of the slap you gave me, she said. Everyone has their own way of making a name for themselves, replied Gunnar, and I won't ask you for long. "You have done wrong and long shall your shame endure," said Ranveig, Gunnar's mother. Gunnar, however, continued to defend himself until his strength failed him, and finally fell after killing two men and almost fatally wounding 16.

Nothing could be made of Gunnar's manslaughter, for he had fallen as an outlaw. But he could be avenged. With this in mind, Skarphedin, one of Nial's sons, went to Gunnar's son Hogne and promised him his help. Hogne rose in the night and took down his father's axe. Ranveig awoke, went up angrily and asked: Who touches the axe that I have forbidden all to take? Hogne replied: I will give it to my father to carry at the Thing in Vallhall. Carry it yourself first, said the grandmother, and avenge your father! Hogne did so, and Gunnar was avenged.

In describing Gunnar's fate, we have had occasion to mention the man who is now the subject of our special attention. We have already come to know him as the wisest man in Iceland, both a man of integrity and a citizen who enjoys universal trust. That man was Nial. We have already mentioned the real reason why we are now turning specifically to his story: that we can learn from it how a most important institution came into being, namely the Court of Five[W] or Fifth Court. So from his story we learn the following: [14]

Nial's sons had come into conflict with a relative of the previously mentioned Gunnar called Thraen Sigfusson, who lived on the Grjotå farm in Fliothshlid. He had once been present when a disgraceful slander was fabricated against Nial and his sons, and from then on they could no longer look upon him with favour. - The dispute continued after their return, and once when Nial's sons came to Thraen to demand compensation, they overheard Halgerde (who lived there with his son) repeating the insulting words of the song in their presence and that of many others. Although Thraen himself had not allowed himself to be insulted, he should still be responsible for what happened in his house. So it came to an open feud between Thraen and the sons of Nial, one of whom, Skarphedin, smashed Thraen's head in two with his axe at Rangå. Nial paid a fine for the manslaughter, and to further atone for the violence, he took Thraen's son Höskuld into his home and treated him as one of his own sons. When he became a man, Nial even wanted to give him a good marriage.

He approached Flose of Svinefjäll, one of the most powerful chieftains in the village and the uncle of Hildigunn, Nial's chosen wife for Höskuld. Flose had no objections, nor did Hildigunn, except that she considered Höskuld to be too insignificant a man, as he had neither a Godord nor a chieftaincy. Nial committed himself for three years, during which time Hildigunn was not to be promised to anyone else. During this time Nial tried everything to get his foster son Höskuld a chieftaincy, but with little success. Finally the Althing was held in the summer of 1003.

This important matter was on the agenda and, as usual, people wanted to hear Nial's advice. But no matter how he spun it, he did not get what he wanted. The following year was no better. So many people were advising that the law should be abandoned in favour of point and edge [as synonyms for spear and sword]. Away with it, said Nial; it is of little use to us to have a lawless society, but it falls to us who know the law to keep the peace. So let us call the chiefs together and consult. They went into Court [15] and Nial said: 'To you, Skapte Thorodson, and to the rest of you chiefs, I would like to point out whether it is not a bad state of our legal system if we are soon taking our matters to the Quarter Court, where they often become so convoluted that it is difficult to find an end to them. It therefore seems to me reasonable and necessary that we should establish a fifth court (Fimtardómr) to hear those cases which cannot be settled by the district courts. He also made suggestions as to how this fifth court should be organised. A few men from each quarter were to form new godords, and anyone who wished to do so was free to submit to them. This Fifth Court was accepted by the legislature and immediately afterwards new godords were formed when Nial asked to be allowed to form one on Hvitanäs for Höskuld. This was granted and Höskuld became a Godordsman. Nothing stood in the way of his union with Hildigunn, and so the wedding took place in Flose.

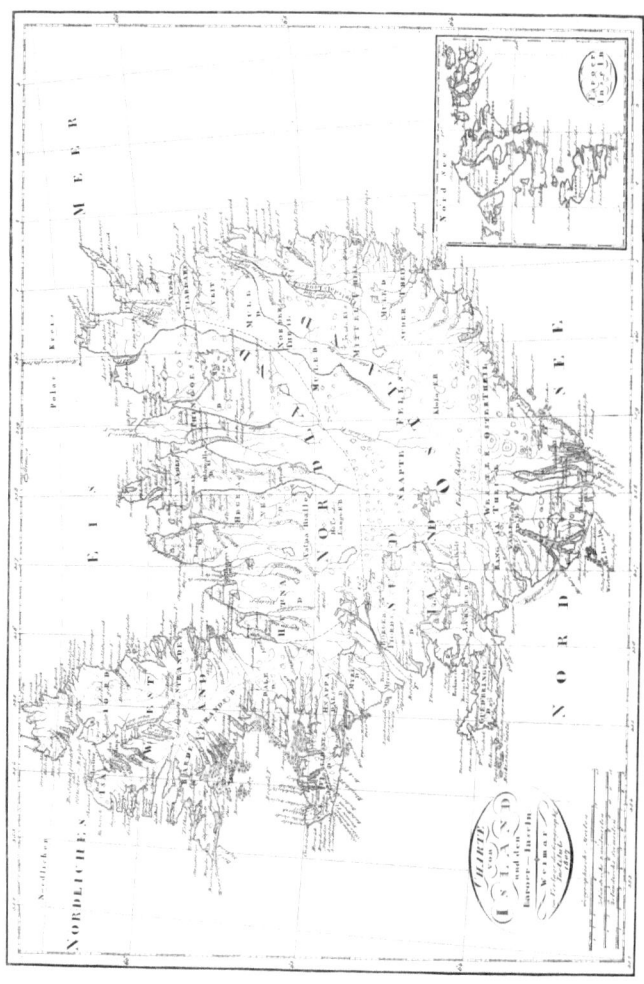

from: Verlag des Geograph. Instituts, „Charte von Island und den Färöer-Inseln", Weimar 1681; Det Kgl. Bibliotek, KBK 1115-0-1807/1, 2021-10-12

So much from the saga of Nial for the origin of the Fifth Court. We will only add the following, partly to complete the picture of the time, partly so that we do not remain ignorant of the fate of this important man. With the decision to establish new Godords and the permission that anyone who wanted to could join them, Mörd had lost his Thingmen at Court, who had joined Höskuld instead. When Mörd's father returned from a journey, he wondered at these changes, and when his son told him what had happened in his absence, he urged him to take revenge, and gave him this advice as his last wish: to cause dissension between Höskuld and the sons of Nial. Mörd succeeded brilliantly, and the matter ended with Höskuld being attacked and killed by Nial's sons. As a result of this act of violence, Nial and the murderers of Flose were brought before the Allthing, whereupon Hildigunn, who had thrown the bloody mantle of Höskuld upon him, made him swear by the power of Christ and all his own manhood and bravery to avenge the dead, or be regarded by all as an outlaw. - At last a fine was agreed upon; but when there was disagreement as to its acceptance, Flose finally kicked the money aside and said that he would not take any of it, not even the smallest part, but that either Höskuld should lie unhappy or his death should be avenged. It was not long before this happened. Flose and his followers gathered and went to Bergthorshvol, where they burned Nial, Bergthora and their sons in the house.

From what we have said above we can see that although there were laws and a legal system, vigilante justice still existed and was the means by which the injured party preferred to seek satisfaction. We also learn how a criminal disturber of the peace was tried before the Althing, but also that crimes were usually paid for with fines or banishment, but that for a life another life was only demanded by a duel [holmgang]. No less does it show us that, like Mörd in Nial's story, it was not beneath one's dignity to falsely incite one's comrades as helpers at the expense of the loss of individuals in order to help regain what had been lost. Nothing was more natural, therefore, than to choose as allies those who were most capable of helping, and that, since patriotism and self-interest went hand in hand, one would not hesitate to consider seeking such allies even outside the fatherland. It should be no surprise that in such a case the first and nearest port of call was Norway, with which one had the closest ties, partly through blood ties and partly through needs. In addition to this, the Norwegian kings[16] did not, when circumstances permitted, neglect any means of keeping Iceland dependent on them - among the most prominent of which were the following: to create dissension among the Icelanders in order to gain an opportunity to interfere in their affairs with the support of the parties, and to win over, by all means of temptation, devoted followers who would see a future advantage In supporting them in their plans to bring the island under their rule. — Add to this the fact that it did not take an extraordinary farsightedness to foresee that not many centuries would remain before an independence that had made itself unworthy of continued existence through egoistic and petty selfishness would perish. It is likely, however, that the very fact that Iceland had a republican constitution hastened the loss of freedom. After all, the same conditions apply everywhere and always. The greater the freedom, the greater the obligation and responsibility not to be unworthy of it. As long as the spirit of a people is such that it will always sacrifice every individual advantage for the common good, as long as it is generous enough to distinguish the true advantages and benefits from the profits of the moment and the advantages of the day, in a word, as long as there is unselfishness of thought, purity of morals, dignity of action, so long can a republican constitution endure. But if the proportions are reversed, a people has indeed forfeited its liberty.

So we are approaching the time when the sun of freedom would set for Iceland. We have pointed out the gradual changes in the character and conditions of the Icelanders. Now, during the last period, civil discord had reached its height. Wealth had accumulated in the hands of certain men who were not content to be chiefs over the Härads and Quartermen who had joined them, but who procured for themselves real, sworn followers to give weight to their will and carry out their orders. That this should result in an endless chain of civil wars is indeed nothing less than unexpected. - The extent to which Norway maintained complete neutrality in this respect can best be learned from the Sturlunga Saga[X], the main part of which we must quote here, both to learn about the life and character of Snorre Sturleson[Y] and for its ability to illuminate Iceland's internal and external conditions at that time, or at the end of the republic[17].

Snorre Sturleson was born in 1178 on the Hwam farm in the Western Quarter. His parents were Sturle Thordson (usually called Hwam-Sturla) and Gudny Bodvarsdotter, both of rather distinguished birth and descended from the Nordic royal houses. At the age of three he entered the house of the scholar Johan Loptson[18, Z], where he remained until the age of 16, acquiring a good knowledge that would later be of great use in the writing of his published works. - As the youngest of three brothers, he had received a rather modest inheritance, while his brothers Sighvat and Thord had become powerful Godes. But what his father's death had left him without, he gained through his marriage to Herdis, the daughter of the wealthy priest Berse of the Borg court[AA], for with her he acquired a considerable fortune. Greedy for goods and money, like his grandfather's father, the famous Gode Snorre, he acquired farm after farm. His fortune grew to such an extent that he was considered the most powerful man in Iceland, with the exception of John Loptson's son Sæmund Johnson. Thus endowed with education and wealth, it was not long before the rank of a Lagman brought him corresponding prestige. In 1213 he was elected Lagman for the whole of Iceland, but continued to be Gode or chief for important districts. He had already begun his career as a writer, and by writing a song in honour of Jarls[BB] Håkan Galin[CC] he gained fame and valuable gifts from the Earl, who even invited him to Norway. He did travel there, but not until 1218, when the death of the Earl [Jarl] and other circumstances forced him to postpone his journey. When he arrived in Norway, he quickly gained the trust and became friends with Skule Jarl^{DD} and the young Håkan Håkansson^{EE}.

He then travelled to Sweden to visit the widow of Håkan Galin, who was married in second marriage to Eskil, the Lagman of Vestergöthland. And the saga tells us that he was given the banner that Knut Ericson carried at the Battle of Gestilren[FF] in the war against King Swerker for a work of Skaldic poetry in her honour. On his return from Vestergöthland to Norway he found the times very different and unfavourable, for Skule Jarl was about to avenge the misdeeds of some Icelanders against some Norwegian merchants[19] and was equipping a fleet for this purpose. Snorre was able to talk the Jarl out of this plan, and he was able to turn the impending danger into a stream of benefits, assuring the Jarl that gifts and honours would bring the Icelanders into submission much more easily than force. Snorre Sturleson returned home with the rank of a Länsman[GG], having promised both redress for the injured and the king's support in carrying out his plans. It is believed that this later promise was actually kept, as he sent his son to Norway after his return in 1220. For it was clearly seen (it was said) that the son was to become the pledge of the father's loyalty. - As for the reason why this promise was not fulfilled, it is perhaps uncertain whether it was lack of ability or lack of will. For, on the one hand, if he had wished to bring his fatherland under Norway, the troubles and quarrels in which he was involved would probably have been a mighty obstacle to its execution. But, on the other hand, we may also suppose, and this will save his honour, that in making such a promise he only wished to give himself an opportunity of getting out of Norway, and to give his countrymen time and space to take the necessary measures. We have mentioned that he was involved in new disturbances and disputes.

If we now add that he owned six farms in the western and southern quarters, which he surrounded with fortifications; that he bound the inhabitants of the whole region by an oath of homage to fight under his banner; that he was, against all constitutions, the chief of four separate godords, and also held shares in several others - if we add all this, we shall see clearly that at one time he allowed himself to be honoured by a whole härad, and at another time he recognised a chief only on condition that he should always fight under him as leader; when we add all this up, we see clearly that the power of constitution had given way to that of wealth, that many a godord had been transformed into a chiefdom of obedience. We can also see that, in the absence of those who opposed the violation of the law, there must at least have been those who could have curbed such power. These opponents, of course, offered everything they could to limit a power that was already well on its way to becoming an autocracy. - But the most dangerous of these were Snorre's own family, his brothers and nephews. In fact, even his own son, Uraekia, was once at odds with him. But the kind of fighting he loved best was setting his enemies against each other and then using their discord to his advantage. For when it came to openly confronting his enemies, he showed little courage. The best proof of this is the fact that when he found himself in a situation that required it, he hastily left for Norway, abandoning the magnificent Reikholt (1230). Those who now took possession of Reikholt were his brother Sighvat and his son Sturla. The latter had met King Hakan in Norway on his way home from Rome, where he had made a pilgrimage, and had made him such promises that they recognised him as Snorre's nephew. - When Snorre arrived, however, there was great tension between Skule Jarl and the king. Snorre joined the former's party and, with his permission to travel, returned home after the death of his brother and nephew which made Reikholt accessible to him again. It was not long, however, before he himself died. After Håkan Håkansson had defeated Skule and the latter had fallen, the king sought Snorre's ruin. The remedy was soon found. On his return Snorre did not give up his old bad habit, but provoked Sighvat's son Tumi in every way to avenge the death of his father and brother on their murderers Kolbein and Gissur, Snorre's own sons-in-law. But of the latter, Gissur was related to King Håkan Håkansson and had been made a Jarl by him. It was to Gissur that the king of Norway turned with the order to either bring Snorre back to Norway as a prisoner or to kill him. It was obvious that the large possessions would make the latter task more attractive. The 63-year-old Snorre was killed during an attack on Reikholt in the night between 22nd and 23rd September 1241.

Thus perished a man who was as great in kindness, learning and wealth as he was in fame and power; indeed, one of the most outstanding men the North has produced; but even if his greatness in this respect cannot be denied, it cannot be overlooked that there were several dark sides to his rich life. - By citing these traits from Snorre's life, we have unrolled a tablet that shows us in the clearest light discord, rapacity, baseness and lust for power. And if these qualities were prevalent in the noblest families of the land, if even Snorre Sturleson cannot be absolved of them, then it should not be surprising or unexpected that they were prevalent among the people as a whole. The rapid decline of the Free State is sure proof that this was indeed the case. No more than 20 years passed between the fall of Snorre and the fall of the Icelandic Republic. By 1261 a large part of the island had already submitted to Norway. By 1264, all of Iceland was under the rule of that kingdom.

We are now at the point where Iceland's independence came to an end and it voluntarily submitted to Norway. This is also the end of our treatise [...].

Specification of sources.

[from the original unchanged, but numbered consecutively]

[1] Schedae c. 3.

[2] Svea Rikes Häfder 1: 190.

[3] Petersen, Danmarks Historie i Hedenold 2: 412.

[4] Landuama S. m. fl.

[5] Petersen 2: 414, 413 ock Geijer Svea Rikes H. 1: 196.

[6] Nordstrom: Bidrag till Svenska samhällsförfattningens historia 1: 4.

[7] Nordström, 1: 7.

[8] Petersen D. H. 2: 523.

[9] Olof Tryggvasons S. C. 80.

[10] Petersen 2: 524 och 526.

[11] Olof Tryggvas. Sag. Cap. 103.

[12] Petersen 2: 488 och följ.

[13] Se Geijer, Sr. Folkets Hist. 1: Cap. 7.

[14] Petersen D. II. 2: 542 o. f.

[15] Nordström, Bidrag t. Sv. S. Hist. 1: 7.

[16] We have already mentioned Olof Tryggvason's intentions. Olof Haraldson involved himself in all kinds

of negotiations and offers, as can be seen from his saga, Cap. 134, 135, 146.

[17] We are hereby following the Geschichte von Dännemark von Dahlman 2: 283. f.

[18] Grandson of Sæmund the Wise, died 1133.

[19] The situation was as follows: In 1216 Sæmund, a grandson of Sæmund the Wise and Snorre Sturleson's foster-brother, had sent his son Paul to Bergen. The inhabitants there, who knew the proud spirit of Sæmund's kinship, received him with joy, saying that he had certainly come there with the intention of becoming their king, or at least count, and then subduing Iceland. Not satisfied with such a reception, he went to Trondheim, but disappeared off its coast. His father, left behind in Iceland, now proceeded against some Bergen merchants who were lying in the Icelandic port of Eyerbacke, as if the inhabitants of Bergen had been his son's murderers, assaulted them and robbed them of part of their cargo. Two merchants from Hardanger were also attacked and robbed.

Trolle's Glossarium.

[added by the translator; all translations from an original, unless otherwise noted, by Albert George Viktorsson Trolle]

A   "**Ingiald Illråde**, Braul Anund's son, was given the byname Illråda, which means "prevailing by acts of violence", or determined, sly in his evil deeds. At his father's grave he swore to increase his kingdom by half on all sides. Those present understood this to mean that this should be done by conquests in honest feud. Ingiald himself, however, understood it differently; for he intended to dispose of the kings of the provinces whose power and possessions limited his own, by cunning or violence. In the night after the funeral feast he therefore burnt down the house in which the celebration had taken place, and there the kings Algoter, his own father-in-law, and Yngvar with his two sons, the kings Sporsnialler and Sigvarter, perished. These were not all, however, but he completed his plan against those who remained, murdered Granmar and Hjorvard, and had King Gudrauder put out of the way by his daughter. Finally, when Ivar moved against him, he held a feast at the royal court of Renninge in Lake Mälar and burned himself, his daughter and his entire court there at night. Apart from that, Ingiald's actions were statecraft according to the taste of the time; but did not stem from a thirst for blood and a desire for harm. Vice versa, they seem to have had their origin in a deeper, calculated plan to achieve unity and strength in leadership. An uncertain tradition also mentions that he had collected the oldest laws of the Uplanders, probably with the intention of making them a general valid law for the whole kingdom. No other features of obstinacy or violence are mentioned during his reign. His burial place is presumed by Sjöborg in his "Collections for Lovers of Antiquities in the North", to be on Fogdö in Lake Mälaren, where Renningeborg was located, as no legend or tradition gives reason to believe that Ingiald's ashes were removed and buried in Gamla Uppsala in a burial mound or elsewhere. Also, one actually finds on Fogdö, on Husby's properties, a so-called king's mound, which can very credibly be regarded as Ingiald's family burial mound. It has a circumference of 360 ells and, like all the tombs of the ancient kings, is surrounded by stone settings and by several smaller mounds in which the members of the court rest."

Berg, Per Gustaf: Art. Ingiald, in: Svenskt Konversations – Lexikon, Second part, Stockholm 1847, p. 247.

At this point, for comparison's sake, we would like to let Snorre Sturleson, one of the protagonists in the present treatise, have his say directly on Ingiald Illråde: (From the Ynglinga saga:)

"On the death of King Ingiald Illråda. Iwar the Widfadme [modern Swedish: "Ingvar den vittfarne", English: "Ingvar the far-travelled", ed. note] came to Skåne after the death of his father-brother King Gudröd, immediately assembled a large army and went up into Sweden. Åsa Illråda had moved home to her father shortly before. King Ingiald was at a banquet at Räninge when he got to know that King Iwar's army had arrived there: Ingiald found then that he was not strong enough to fight Iwar, and he knew exactly what would happen to him if he fled: namely, that his enemies would come from everywhere and attack him. Then King Ingiald and his daughter Åsa made the decision, which afterwards became very well known, that they got their entourage quite drunk and then set fire to the king's hall, which burned down with everyone inside, including King Ingiald and Åsa.

This is what Thiodolfer says:

"And Ingiald,

On Räninge,

Trampled alive

By the smoke's raiser (fire);

As the friend of the houses and of Tyr (fire)

With glowing soles

The divine king

Trampled through.

And this king

Seemed to be generally

Rare

Among the Swedes;

Since he was the first

Who would himself

Have his quick life

shortened."

Sturleson, Snorre [unnamed translator into Swedish]: Konunga-Sagor, Stockholm 1816, [First part] p. 58-59.

"**Thiodolfer** af Hwin (Hwen)" or Thiodolfer of the "Hwinverski or Hwenverske [...] (of Hwen)" [today the island of Ven between Denmark and Sweden, editor's note].

ale, Historisk tidskrift för Skåneland, Nr 3 1979, Hallberg, Göran: Ven — klippor, skum och scharlakan, p. 17.

B   "**Harald Hårfager**, whose reign is thought to have been around 863. [...] **Thiodolfer** is Thiodolfer den Hwimwerke, a skald at the time of Harald Hårfager, and this king's most loyal friend, who lived on the island of Hwen, [...]".

Bunge, Dr. F. G. v. (Ed.): Archiv für die Geschichte Liv-, Esth- und Curlands, vol. IV, Dorpat [Tartu] 1845, p. 148.

Harald I. Hårfager, one of the most distinguished kings in Norway, son of Halfdan III the Black, became, according to Sh. Rosenhane [Baron Schering

Rosenhane, among other things Swedish resident at the peace negotiations in Münster in 1648, ed. note], sole king around 854, according to other accounts in 898, whose descendants ruled in Norway until 1319, when the last prince of the Ynglinga dynasty, Hakon V. Magnusson, died. At the time of his father's death, Harald was staying on Dovrefjell and had already shown great bravery and outstanding qualities in several battles. Love made him a conqueror. He had offered his hand to Gyda, a Danish king's daughter; but the proud princess answered Harald's envoy that she would not become his wife until he was master of all Norway. Harald then swore that he would neither cut nor comb his hair until Gydas' wish was fulfilled, and ten years after that he was lord over his whole fatherland. In the meantime, his hair had become very long and because he did not take care of it, it took on a very shabby appearance, which is why he was nicknamed Harald Cap. After he had started to care for it again, it became exceptionally beautiful, and he was therefore called Harald Hårfager [Beautiful Hair, ed. note]. Harald is said to have died in 938, having brought his kingdom into a flourishing state by wise laws and the promotion of trade.

Berg, Per Gustaf: Art. Harald I Hårfager, in: Svenskt Konversations – Lexikon, Second part, Stockholm 1847, p. 56.

C   Gardar   Svafarsson   --->   Gardarsholm, oldest name of Iceland. Around 860, Gardar, the son of a Swede named Svafar who lived on Zealand, wanted to sail to the Hebrides, but was driven off to the east coast of Iceland by a storm. By following the coast, he then sailed around the island. On the north side, at a place afterwards called Husavik, he built some houses to spend the winter in. A man who had come along on the voyage settled near Husavik, but Gardar himself sailed back and came to Norway. He greatly praised the land he discovered, which was later called Gardarsholm, but this name was soon replaced by the increasingly common name of Iceland.

Expeditionen af Nordisk familjebok: Art. Gardarsholm, in: Nordisk familjebok, Fifth volume, Stockholm 1882, pp. 881-882.

D   On a trial basis, **Ingolf** and **Leif** also went there in 871 and landed in a bay on the east coast. They explored the country and returned the following spring to prepare for their emigration. But the effort fell on Ingolf alone, for Leif went to Ireland, plundered there and took slaves and other booty. In 874 they finally left Norway on two ships. On one Ingolf sailed with their joint possessions, on the other Leif, who in the meantime had married Helga, with his Irish booty. Thus Ingolf and Leif became Iceland's first settlers or, as it was called in Iceland, land namers (land takers).

Hildebrand Hildebrand, Hans Olof: Lifvet på Island under sagotiden, Stockholm 1867, p. 4.

E   **Are vise** or **frode** [Are Torgilsson, called "den vise" or "frode", i.e. "the wise one", ed.] was the first to write down the history of Iceland and describe the most important events on the island. His Book of Icelanders is still in existence and begins thus: "I first wrote the Book of Icelanders for our bishops Thorlak and Kettil and showed it to these two and to the priest Sämund. But as they thought it good to have it or even to expand it, I wrote this and added what came to my knowledge afterwards. If something is false, one should rather take what is found to be truer." His book deals with the most important events on the island, all of which, with one exception, I have mentioned or alluded to in the foregoing -- about the land-namers, the introduction of laws, the establishment of the Althing, the counting of time -- in 970 a change was made in the former way of reckoning the years -- about the division of the quarters, the settlement of Greenland, the introduction of Christianity, the foreign bishops, and the first two to be born in Iceland, Isleif and Gissor. He ends with the year 1120. "Here ends this book," it says.

Hildebrand Hildebrand, Hans Olof: Lifvet på Island under sagotiden, Stockholm 1867, p. 146.

F   Erik Gustaf Geijer

Born: 1783-01-12 - Ransäter parish, Värmlands Län.
Death: 1847-04-23 - Jakob parish, Stockholms Län

Author, historian, poet, composer

Erik Gustaf Geijer, https://sok.riksarkivet.se/sbl/artikel/12976, Svenskt biografiskt lexikon (art av Elsa Norberg), Accessed 2021-05-23.

G   From the earliest times, the division of the land with regard to the administration of justice was called

"**Härad**". Härad is the same term as "hundari" and means an association of hundreds. Initially it was an association for warlike purposes. After a more settled way of life had been adopted, the name "härad" continued to be used for the individual legal communities within the provinces (landscapes). Actually, the name belongs to the laws of the Goethans (Goths), and hundari, on the other hand, occurs among the Svear tribes. The founding of new settlements in the wilderness was called the building of härads. The term "härad" was originally personal and referred to the families that made up the community; but gradually changed to a term for the land itself that they cultivated. [...]

Berg, Per Gustaf: Art. Härad, in: Svenskt Konversations – Lexikon, Second part, Stockholm 1847, p. 206.

H However, there were courts in Iceland before the Althing was introduced. The Goden's duties also included speaking at the public meetings that naturally took place at the house of the gods (temple) he was in charge of. [...] Iceland is divided by fairly clear natural boundaries into four areas, which were named after the compass direction or the main settlement of the area. In each quarter there were to be three subdivisions with judicial parishes, each with its own court, and in each such area three **Godords**. In the North Country this arrangement could not be agreed to, but a fourth judicial parish was established, and so there were twelve Godords there. The Godords included in this distribution therefore had complete administrative significance. However, even after this, anyone could build up a court and become its Gode, but this value was then of a completely individual nature and had no influence whatsoever on the administration.

Hildebrand Hildebrand, Hans Olof: Lifvet på Island under sagotiden, Stockholm 1867, pp. 82-83.

I   On the Lon farm in the south-eastern part of Iceland lived an emigrant, **Ulfljot**. He had come out late and when he found the land ahead cultivated, he bought the farm in question. It was he who created the laws of Iceland. One does not know the closer circumstances that preceded this remarkable event. It is probable that some of the most respected men in the country, such as the Godes, approached the newcomer and asked him to write a code of laws; otherwise the readiness with which the new laws were adopted cannot be explained. Ulfljot accepted the commission, although he had already managed to reach the age of sixty, and went to Norway to draw up a law proposal in consultation with his mother-brother [uncle, ed.] Thorleif the Wise.

Hildebrand Hildebrand, Hans Olof: Lifvet på Island under sagotiden, Stockholm 1867, p. 79.

J   **Althingi** is the nation's oldest institution, and the highest. Its foundation at Thingvellir (Parliament Plains) in 930 AD marks the birth of the Icelandic nation. Althingi was an assembly of the nation, where the leading chieftains met to discuss various matters. Althingi passed legislation and dispensed justice. Althingi assembled around the middle of June for a session of about two weeks, and all free and law-abiding citizens could attend. Those attending the assembly dwelt in temporary camps known as búdir during the session. Sanctuary during the session was intended to ensure freedom to observe the proceedings. Althingi was well-attended, as it was the centre of power and interaction.

Althingi, in: (Ed.) Administration of Althingi, Reykjavík 2018, p. 6.

following page:

Sketch of Thingvellir, looking north along Almannagjá ("All Men's Gorge") towards Lögberg (Law Rock), reproduced by the editor from a photo taken by Viktor Meyer (Halstenbek) in 1973.

Lögberg

Thingvellir

K "The **Lagman** was, as his title indicates, a man of the law [lag] who had to know and be familiar with what had been law and custom in the country from times gone by. In Sweden he was at the same time what was called Lögsögumadr in Iceland, because it was his duty to sometimes tell the people the law according to which they had to obey. It is understandable that a man who knew the old laws better than anyone else was best qualified to pass judgement in cases that had not occurred in the past. It is understandable that a man to whom one turned with confidence in legal matters also gained significant influence in other respects."

Hildebrand Hildebrand, Hans Olof (Translation to German J. Mestorf): Das heidnische Zeitalter in Schweden, Hamburg 1873, p. 208.

L **Olaf Tryggvason,** in full Olaf I Tryggvason, (born *c.* 964—died *c.* 1000), Viking king of Norway (995–*c.* 1000), much celebrated in Scandinavian literature, who made the first effective effort to Christianize Norway. Olaf, the great-grandson of the Norwegian king Harald I Fairhair and the son of Tryggvi Olafsson, a chieftain in southeastern Norway, was born soon after his father was killed by the Norwegian ruler Harald II Graycloak. According to legend, Olaf fled with his mother, Astrid, to the court of St. Vladimir, grand prince of Kiev and of all Russia, and was trained as a Viking warrior. In 991 he joined in the Viking attacks on England, which were resumed with the accession of Ethelred II the Unready to the English throne in 978. Ethelred sued for peace in 991, agreeing to pay large sums in tribute, and again when Olaf invaded with the Danish king Sweyn I Forkbeard in 994.

Already a Christian, Olaf was confirmed at Andover (in modern Hampshire) in 994, with Ethelred, with whom he had been reconciled, as his godfather. Learning of the growing revolt against the Norwegian king Haakon the Great, Olaf returned to Norway and was accepted as king on Haakon's death in 995. He forcefully imposed Christianity on the areas under his control, the coast and the western islands, but had little influence elsewhere. By commissioning missionaries and baptizing visiting dignitaries, Olaf was able to introduce Christianity to the Shetland, Faroe, and Orkney islands and to Iceland and Greenland. (Christianity was adopted by the Icelandic parliament [Althing] about 1000). Despite his religious zeal, however, he failed to establish lasting religious (or administrative) institutions in Norway.

Olaf met his death in the Battle of Svolder (*c.* 1000) at the hands of the Danish king Sweyn I, the Swedish king Olaf Skötkonung, and Eric the Norwegian, earl of Lade. The battle is often retold in medieval Scandinavian poems. After his death large portions of Norway reverted to foreign rule.

Britannica, The Editors of Encyclopaedia. "Olaf Tryggvason".
Encyclopedia Britannica, Invalid Date,
https://www.britannica.com/biography/Olaf-Tryggvason. Accessed 24 May 2021.

M "[...] King Olav Trygvason sent **Stefner Thorgilsson**, likewise Thangbrand a Saxon, his court preacher, to this island [Iceland] in 996. [...]"

Ioensen, Finnur: Historia ecclesiastica Islandiae (Translator unknown), in: Zugabe zu den Göttingischen Anzeigen von gelehrten Sachen unter der Aufsicht der königl. Gesellschaft der Wissenschaften, The first volume, Göttingen 1777, p. 277.

N " [...] Occasional missions to Iceland in the later 10th century are recorded, but little progress was made until Olaf I Tryggvason, king of Norway, sent out the German priest **Thangbrand** *c.* 997. Thangbrand was a ruthless, brutal man; he was outlawed and returned to Norway *c.* 999. But in the year after Thangbrand left (*c.* 1000), the Icelandic parliament (Althingi) resolved, at the instigation of King Olaf, that all should be baptized, [...]"

Britannica, The Editors of Encyclopaedia. "The end of paganism". Encyclopedia Britannica, Invalid Date, https://www.britannica.com/history/The end of paganism. Accessed 24 May 2021.

O **Gissur,** a common name in one of Iceland's best-known large farming families, the Mosfellings, later the Haukadalings.

- 1st stem father. G. Teitsson Hviðe [the white one, ed.] at Mosfell (near Reykjavik), was, just like Hjalte Skeggjason, leader of the movement that led to the adoption of Christianity by the Althing (around the year 1000).

— - 2. G. Isleifsson, the grandson of the former, succeeded his father Isleif, the first native-born bishop of Iceland (1056), in the episcopate and ruled Iceland for 36 years (1082-1118) as if he had been a king (Adam of Bremen). He was, so Are Frode tells us, so popular with the people that for his sake, after the advice of Sämund Frode and Markus Lögsöguman, it was laid down by law that every individual should count and value his goods, both land and movable property, and swear that they were valued correctly, and thereupon give a tenth of them. This took place in 1096 and is rightly regarded by Are as significant evidence of the people's obedience to G.. The Althing also decided that Skalholt's farm and church - G.'s own inheritance - should be made the bishop's seat, and additionally provided it with large donations of movable property. When the inhabitants of northern Iceland wanted to obtain their own bishop, G. renounced the revenues of the northern quarter for the establishment of the bishopric of Hola (1106), thus making the collegiate division of Iceland as it remained during the Catholic period. On G.'s initiative, the first census in the lands of the north was conducted - probably on the occasion of the introduction of tithing - according to which there were 4,440 peasants in Iceland, i.e. farm owners who owed taxes. G.'s brother Teit inherited the farm Haukadal (near Geysir) from his foster father Hall

Thorarinsson, which then became the family's principal seat. [...]

Expeditionen af Nordisk familjebok: Art. Gissur, in: Nordisk familjebok, Fifth volume, Stockholm 1882, pp. 1224-1225.

P   Njål (Njal), in full Njal Thorgeirsson, Icelandic great landowner, protagonist of the "Njåls Saga", born c. 935, lived on the farm of Bergtorsvall on the south coast and is mentioned in the saga as an attractive and very knowledgeable man of the law. He was so wise that he could see into the future, and also upright, though not without a certain cunning in his advice. With his wife Bergtora he had sons Skarphedin, Grim and Helge, of whom the first-named especially excelled in all manly skills. N. had a good relationship with his neighbour Gunnar on Hliðarendi and even managed to maintain it despite the violence of his own sons and the antipathy between Bergtora and Gunnar's wife Hallgerd. After Gunnar's death (993), however, he did not succeed in preventing the outbreak of the feud in which many of the most distinguished families were involved and which ended with a raid on Bergtorsvall, in which N., his wife and his sons lost their lives (on 3 Septembcr 1011). N. was the one who enforced the establishment of the Fifth Court as the highest court in Iceland (1004), and was also one of the first to adopt Christian doctrine.

The saga of Njål is one of the Icelandic sagas that many consider to be the most important in terms of style and composition, as well as in terms of characterisation and richness of content. The saga, which revolves around the landowner Njål Thorgeirsson (see previous article) and his family, depicts events from the southern part of Iceland in the second half of the tenth century and the beginning of the eleventh century. Many facts about the legal system on the island are given in the saga, but recent criticism has shown it to be unreliable on several points. The story was last and best published in Copenhagen in 1875; […].

Expeditionen af Nordisk familjebok: Art. Njål, in: Nordisk familjebok, Eleventh volume, Stockholm 1887, p. 1171.

Q **Fljotshlid** is a beautiful farming district in Southern Iceland. It is one of the main sites for Njal's Saga, a masterpiece of the saga literature. It is surrounded by some of the most active and best known volcanoes in the world.

These volcanoes are Hekla (north), Katla (east), Eyjafjallajokull (south) and the Westman Islands (south west, and including Surtsey, that was formed in the eruption of 1963-67). Markarfljot river passes between Fljotshlid and Eyjafjallajokull.

Gunnar Hamundarson, main hero of Njal's Saga, lived in the area, at the farm Hlidarendi. It is said that when he had been sentenced to exile and was about to leave, he looked back at the Fljotshlid hill and proclaimed that because of the beauty of the scene he would not leave and hence rode back to face his fate.

Poet Thorsteinn Erlingsson lived in the area, as did artist Nina Tryggvadottir and Tomas Saemundsson, the latter active in the 19th century fight for independence.

"Fljótshlíð Travel Guide". Guide to Iceland, 25.05.21, https://guidetoiceland.is/travel-iceland/drive/fljotshlid. Accessed 26 May 2021.

R   Bergþórshváll

Large farm approx. 5 km inland from Landeyjasandur on road 252.

"Die Örtlichkeiten der Njáls saga ". Universität Leipzig, [no date], https://home.uni-leipzig.de/histspra/WS17-18Homepage/04-040-2003Vor-undFrühstufen /MaterialienAltnordisch/Text2Njalssaga/Njalssaga-Orte.pdf. Accessed 26 May 2021.

S   The **year 984** falls in a phase of climate warming that is also referred to as the "Medieval Optimum". Nevertheless, temperature curves of the Northern Hemisphere derived from multi-proxy and tree-ring reconstructions indicate clear fluctuations also into the negative, i.e. colder, range for the years before the turn of the millennium. Ice cores from a depth of between 309.85 and 311.585 metres, equivalent to the period between the years 980 and 987 AD, obtained from the Greenland Ice Shield, show a significant fluctuation for this period in the leading isotopes according to which the temperature curves are reconstructed. It is therefore probable that the external temperatures of the northern hemisphere fluctuated at this time and thus a preceding bad harvest year of 983 implied in the text is at least not excluded.

according to: Kobashi, T., J.P. Severinghaus, J.-M. Barnola, K. Kawamura, T. Carter, and T. Nakaegawa. 2010. Persistent multi-decadal Greenland temperature fluctuation through the last millennium. Climatic Change, Vol. 100, pp. 733-756. DOI 10.1007/s10584-009-9689-9

T **Träldomen** / Slavery / Servitude in the North. Our pagan forefathers dragged home captives, as many as they could accommodate on their Viking ships, from the coasts of the Baltic, from England, Scotland and Ireland, from Germany, France and even Spain; they took men, women and children of all ranks, monks and priests, youths and maidens of noblest birth, the daughters of kings and earls.

Prisoners of war were thus the first, most general, and most common source of slavery in the North. The second was that children born of slaves remained in the status of their parents and belonged to the class of slaves. Nevertheless, our provincial laws differed from those of other peoples in the mild provision that the child followed the better side, that is, it was free, if either the father or the mother belonged to the free, for it was believed not only that the womb impregnated and freed, but also that a free-born man who begot a child with a female slave transferred his freedom to the latter; but he had to solemnly acknowledge in court the same child as his, so that no dispute might arise in the future about its being freeborn, and, moreover, if the slave was not his own but belonged to someone else, it was his duty to compensate her master both for the loss he suffered from the slave's reduced capacity to work in her pregnant state and for the cost of bringing up the child as long as it remained in the master's house where it was born. House-born slaves, trained from childhood in the rustic work of the house and accustomed to perform it with care and fidelity, had a great advantage over the others and were called fostre because they had been brought up and educated in the master's house. Even free men were sometimes placed in the class of slaves if they had either accumulated greater debts than they could pay, or committed dishonourable offences which revealed a low and disgraceful disposition, such as one expected to find only among serfs, but not among free-born men, and in this case it was thought proper to put them in the same condition to which their conduct belonged. Thieves, therefore, became the servants of the robbed, unless they were able to reconcile him with a fine, or to pay his damages; and the debtor, who could not do right for himself in any other way, became the slave of his creditor, until he had paid off his debt by labour, or by the help of his relatives. Severe hardship and poverty in crop failure years, inability and the failure to make a living in any other way, sometimes even hatred of relatives, drove one or the other to sell their freedom and submit to the property of a householder in order to obtain shelter and bread or to deprive the heirs of the property by transferring the heir to the one into whose care they placed themselves, for the householder had a right to all the property of the slave. These were called "Gäfträlar" ["gäf" or "gäv": something that is given, a gift; in German then roughly Gaben-Sklaven or

Gebsklaven; in English today perhaps to be translated as gift-slaves, ed. note], because they had voluntarily given themselves into servitude. They belonged to the most detested class of slaves, because the northerners assumed that those who thus voluntarily disposed of the status of free-born men and sold their most valuable possessions were either of a fundamentally low and dishonourable mind, or of the highest degree foul, which is why the manslaughter of such a slave could be punished with three marks, while the manslaughter of other slaves was punished with three to four marks, and that of house-born slaves with eight weighed or appraised marks.

The price for a slave also varied greatly. Thus a gift-slave was valued at 24 lots [fineness, ed. note] of silver, another slave at 48, and home-born slaves at 128 lots. In contrast to other indwelling servants, the slaves were called forced servants [in the Swedish original "Annödughshjon": from "annödga" → early New High German "annötigen" → to force someone to do something; "hjon": generally household member, specifically servants, service people, editor's note], as those whose lot was the most miserable of all. They were employed, each according to his physical strength, ability and skill, to do all the tasks on the farm, in the fields and in the forest. As a rule, they were given the heaviest and most difficult jobs and those that others considered humiliating for themselves. They herded the cattle, chopped up firewood, burned coal and extracted salt.
The female slaves, called "ambat" in the ancient nordic language, performed the tasks required in the house

and in the barn; grinding flour and baking bread are named in the ancient sagas as work that certainly belonged to them. The most skilled and best-behaved of the slaves, especially among the home-born, were made overseers over the others, were appointed heads of farms, and sometimes even half-farmers. Such bore the appellation of "Bryti", as those who gave work and food to the others. "Konungsbryti" ["konung" = king, ed.] were therefore called those who presided over the royal courts, for slaves were not seldom or originally taken to these and other such services, which is why the positions were long despised by the free, at least by those who placed a high value on their freedoms and independence.

Responsible to the bryti was the "dajan", the one of the slave women who had supervision over the others or who presided over the internal house management on a farm. Over his slaves the lord of the house possessed such unrestricted power that even at the end of the thirteenth century, although Christianity had already gained a foothold and customs had been greatly toned down, a lord of the house, his wife and his children could punish a slave with death or ill-treat him as they pleased, without the law granting itself any power to impose the slightest fine on them for it. It is not uncommon in the sagas to hear of skinned [meaning here: given open wounds by blows, the skin is stripped off ("hudstruken") at the places where they were beaten, ed.] house maids, and "slave-beating" was the term used when someone had been beaten so badly that they lay on the floor with broken bones and disfigured so that they could not move from the spot. The laws provided that a slave should at best be bought through a broker and with a witness, and if bad habits or a vice of the slave were concealed by the seller, the latter was declared obliged to compensate the damage that could thereby be caused to the buyer at any time. One made gifts with slaves, one could give them away as a fine, one treated them in everything the same as other property, but an improper cohabitation between their slaves was not permitted by our forefathers. The slave had to properly unite with a woman, and this was to be done with the permission of the landlord; then he was considered a married man, but since the children born of such marriages did not belong to their parents but to the landlord, and a serf could not exercise any paternal or household power, the marriage of serfs did not have the same prestige as that of freemen, which is why the married servant is not called a husband in the laws but a "Kapsir". The same right that the master of the house had over the slave himself, he also had over the slave's property, so that everything the slave owned or acquired in the master's service belonged to the master, which is why even in our landscape laws slaves are put on the same level as beggars, and if relatives wanted to ransom a relative from servitude, they had to swear that the ransom came from their own money and not from that of the slave, because otherwise the master would take his own property as ransom for the slave. From the fact that the slave was regarded in all respects as the unconditional property of the landlord, over which the state could acquire no rights, it naturally followed that the slave had no obligations to the general public or to society.

He had no civil rights, could testify to nothing, was not allowed to bear arms, was not subject to law and justice with other men, he was not the holder of personal peace and security as a free [male, ed.] citizen, not the holder of a higher inviolability, had for himself no secured protection by law, no protection by the general public, which is why making someone a slave was also called depriving someone of his personal peace.

But because the slave stood outside any relation to society, and was regarded no differently from a thing which belonged by unrestricted right to its owner, it was incumbent on the latter to answer for all his acts, so that if the slave committed theft or murder, or otherwise behaved violently either towards a free man or his slave, it fell to the master of the house to expiate the offence with a fine, because he had not "tamed his slave better".

If he refused to do so, preferring instead to hand over the offender to be killed or punished by the claimant at his will, then the slave was hung with an oak rod around his neck on the gatepost by the landlord's courtyard; where the corpse was to hang until the rod had rotted, and a fine of forty marks hit anyone who dared to cut off the rod. The intention was to force the master of the house to pay a fine rather than hand over the slave, because people despised taking revenge on such a monster and therefore mainly demanded fines for crimes committed by slaves. Misdeeds committed against other men's slaves were not considered to have been committed against them, but were judged only according to the damage that the landlord suffered as a result, so that if a slave was beaten to death or otherwise inflicted an injury so that he became incapacitated, no penalty was imposed other than full compensation for the value of the slave, in order to relieve the landlord. In general, slaves were held in such deep contempt that among the swear words, the term "slave" was one of the most insulting, so that it was punishable by such fines if someone abusively referred to a man born into a family as a freed slave or accused him of sodomy, and dying by the hands of slaves was considered one of the most shameful ways of dying. In general, the slaves of the ancient inhabitants of the North were treated with a certain degree of humanity, although it happened now and then that a master who was the absolute master of his slave's life punished him too harshly in anger and heat of temper. Even the laws provided for a fatherly upbringing of the children of slave women, for if a landlord wished to prove his right to a home-born slave, he had to swear by witnesses and a twelve-man oath [an oath to be taken by twelve free men, ed. note] and certify that the slave was born in his house, had drunk milk from his mother's breast, was clothed and placed in a cradle. As often as our ancestors celebrated solemn occasions at merry drinking parties, at sacrificial feasts, engagements, weddings and invitations to honour the deceased, blessings and joy were also shared with slaves. Assaults against them at these merry feasts were punishable by the same fine in the laws as assaults against freeborn men. It was intended that the slave should also enjoy some refreshment from his work, that he too should have his moments of joy and happiness in life, and the moments of happiness should be as peaceful for him as for the free man. Good farmers not only allowed their slaves opportunities to work for profit, but also enabled them to buy their way out of slavery with the money they had saved and earned. A sense of humanity and a loftiness of thought unexpected in those times not seldom shine forth from the actions of our forefathers. In this way the condition of many slaves was eased, so that although the Scandinavian inhabitant of the north looked down on these creatures with proud contempt, in accordance with the high value he attached to freedom, the fate of the slave in the north was nevertheless more bearable than in many other countries. For this reason, even in the old sagas, slaves often appear with traits of noble devotion to their landlords, and many a slave gained his freedom as a gift for proven loyalty and efficiency or for having shown courage.

The landlord, or the one who, with the good will of the landlord, ransomed the slave, then brought him to court, publicly announced that all rights applied to him as a free man, accepted him into his clan, which was called "introducing him into the clan", and thus took responsibility for his behaviour in society. After that, the freed man could decide for himself and answer for himself, as well as take the oath. But he was still under the supervision or in a certain dependence on his previous master, and in case he behaved ungratefully or disrespectfully towards him, he became a slave again as punishment for this. The son of the released man, too, if he offended in the same way against his father's former master or the latter's son, had to pay again the ransom paid by his father as a reconciliation. It was not believed that the one who did not know how to behave freely and with decency in domestic relations could be a good fellow citizen.

Those who were freed formed a subordinate class of free men. According to the ancients, the transition from slavery to freedom should be gradual, which is why the freedman's children were also better regarded and respected than the father. As Christianity became more accepted, slavery finally began to disappear. Birger Jarl forbade the use of given slaves, Thorkel Knutsson restricted slavery, and when Magnus Eriksson in 1335 made his sovereign tour ["Eriksgata", i.e. Eriks Road or tour of the sovereign was the name given to the journey that the newly elected Swedish kings in the Middle Ages had to make through the various counties in order to be confirmed by the law men of the counties. Ed. note] on horseback, slavery was abolished altogether, so that it was strictly forbidden to call anyone a slave or slave girl.

Berg, Per Gustaf: Art. Träldomen i norden, in: Svenskt Konversations – Lexikon, Fourth part, Stockholm 1851, pp. 114-116.

U   „[...] We have examples of this in the Gode Geir and in Gizur the White (hviti), who, accompanied by eighty men, attacked Gunnar of Hlidarende alone in his dwelling, and, after part of their men had been wounded and part killed, would have had to stop the attack, if the Gode Geir had not discovered through his cleverness that Gunnar lacked ammunition. [...]"

Wilhelmi, Karl: Island, Hvitramannaland, Grönland und Vinland oder der Norrmänner Leben auf Island und Grönland und deren Fahrten nach Amerika schon über 500 Jahre vor Columbus, Heidelberg 1842, pp. 96-97.

V   **Rangá**, a river in southwest Iceland.

Mentioned several times in the Njals Saga.

Rangárvellir, the area between ýtri Rangá and Eytri Rangá.

Foregoing drawing taken from: Iceland – Its Volcanoes, Geysers and Glaciers by Charles S. Forbes: view „Hekla from Rangaa", London 1860, p. 266

W   "[...] After this, the land was divided into quarters, so that there were three "Things" in each quarter, and the people obliged to attend the "Thing" were each had to pursue their affairs in their own quarter; however, four "Things" were appointed in the northern quarter, because there was no other way of arranging the matter, for those who lived north of Eyafiord did not want to attend the "Thing" there, nor did those who lived west of Eyafiord want to attend the "Thing" in Skagafiord. In the meantime, they were not to provide more judges from that quarter and not more to the Althings court (lógretta) than from any of the other quarters. Thereupon, the quadripartite or Quarter Thing [or quadripartite court] was instituted. So Ulfhedin, Gunnar's son, the lawman, told us. [...] "

Dahlmann, Dr. E. F.: Forschungen auf dem Gebiete der Geschichte, Altona 1822, p. 469.

Four quarterly courts (fjórungsdómar) were held at the Althing, one for each quarter of the country. The number of judges in each **quarter court** was 9, appointed at the beginning of the Althing by the Godes of the quarter from the ranks of their Thingmen present at the Thing. Finally, there was a supreme court, the Fifth Court (fimtardomr), consisting of 12 men from each quarter appointed by the Godes, 48 in all, but only 36 of whom were to participate in the decision, so that each of the parties could exclude six judges.

Generally, one could choose to sue in the quarter court

instead of the court of the district to which the defendant belonged. If the case was brought before the district court and decided unanimously there, the case was finally settled. However, if the decision was not unanimous, the case must be brought before the quarter court instead. A similar regulation applied to the quarter court, where, if no unanimity was reached, the case had to be referred to the fifth court, where the case was then decided by majority vote. It could therefore happen that a case went through all three instances. Except in the case mentioned, neither the quarter court nor the fifth court was to be an appellate court, and a counterbalance to the appeal on grounds of disagreement was sought by requiring the judges of the district courts and the quarter court to take an oath of disagreement (vefangseiðr) in the event of a disagreement; those who were of the same opinion sat down together, and both parties declared what judgment they would give and the reasons for it, and invited each other to join in the opinion they held. Both parties then gave their respective judgments on the matter. The case had then to be brought before the higher court if both the plaintiff and the defendant accused the judges of the other of having judged unlawfully and fined them. There were no legal remedies in the Fifth Court and no connection between it and the Legislative Assembly; namely, nowhere is there any mention of a case being referred from the Fifth Court - or from the other courts - to the Legislative Assembly; incidentally, the Fifth Court was seated in the same place as the Legislative Assembly, i.e. on its benches.

Finsen, Vilhjálmur Ludvig: Om de islandske Love i Fristatstiden, Kjøbenhavn 1873, p. 53.

X   Sturla   Thordsson,   nephew   of   Snorre Sturleson, was well known in his time both in Iceland and Norway. He is the author of the Sturlunga saga, at least in large parts, which contains the history of his own clan and Iceland in the twelfth and up to the middle of the thirteenth century. He even composed a song in honour of Birger Jarl.

Berg, Per Gustaf: Art. Strula Thordsson, in: Svenskt Konversations – Lexikon, Third Part, Stockholm 1848, p. 764.

Y   Snorre Sturleson [Snorri Sturluson], the of the Old North widely known historical author, was born in 1179 into a clan which derived its origins from both the Ynglinga clan and the Lodbrok clan, and was raised by Jon Loptson, who was the grandson of Sämund hin Frode and King Magnus Barfot of Norway.

Snorre Sturleson became the wisest, richest and most powerful Icelander of his time, and took a most unfortunate, sometimes for him not honourable, role between the many quarrelling factions that divided the more powerful families of the island at that time. Not seldom did he come to the Althing at the head of nearly a thousand armed men. In 1218 he visited Norway for the first time and Sweden the following year, where he was warmly received by the Göta Lagman Eskil and his wife Christina, who had previously been married to the Norwegian Jarl Hakan

Galin, in whose honour Snorre Sturleson had written a Skald poem. Now he wrote such a poem also for Christina and received from her, among other gifts, the banner that King Erik Knutsson had carried in the war against Sverker the Younger. Later, he even wrote a poem in praise of King Erik Läspe. In Norway, he became King Håkan's drost [one of the highest officials in the kingdom] and Länsmann [see Glossarium GG "Länsmann", editor's note].

On his second visit to Norway in 1237, he was elevated to the rank of Jarl by Duke Skule, but is best known as Lagman in Iceland, an office he held several times with great distinction. Soon after his elevation to Jarl he fell out of favour with King Håkan, and this, on his return to Iceland, gave rise to the outbreak of intrigues by his enemies. Gissor Thorvaldson, who had formerly been his son-in-law, now appointed Jarl by King Håkan, had him attacked and murdered at his farm Reikholt, on the night of 22 September 1241. Such was the end of the well-known Snorre Sturleson in his 63rd year.

A friend, who had become aware of the secret intrigue against his [Snorre's] life, is said to have sent him a warning letter the day before, but this is said to have been composed, so that it could not be read by anyone, with so-called turning or binding runes, and that so strangely that even the wise Struleson could not decipher it and thus not escape his impending fate. In the Icelandic annals he is credited with the writing or compilation of the younger Edda, and it is said of him that he was a wise and learned man, a great and clever chieftain. The outstanding Nordic royal sagas written by him, sometimes called "Heims Kringla" after the first words of the preface, are rightly counted among the best historical works from all times and in all languages, and represent the main source of knowledge about the whole of the North's oldest early times.

Berg, Per Gustaf: Art. Sturleson, Snorre, in: Svenskt Konversations –
Lexikon, Third Part, Stockholm 1848, pp. 764 et seq..

Z   "[...] that he enjoyed an excellent education in his youth, in that he happened to be brought up from his third year by the chief **John Loptson**, who lived on the farm Odda under the present Rangerwalle Syssel in the South Country, as a result of a dispute that Snorre's father Sturla had with the priest Paul Solvsson at Reikholt, which dispute John Loptson settled. This man's paternal grandfather was the famous priest and collector of Eddic songs Sämund Sigfusson, called hinn Fróði, the scholar, and his mother Thora was a daughter of the Norwegian king Magnus Barfod.

This chief was considered in his time the most learned, wise, and at the same time the richest man in Iceland, and he led a splendor corresponding to his great fortune. He was a rare man in every respect; for his noble heart matched his great intellect and learning. His house was a true school of science. Here our Snorre, who lost his father when he was only five years old, spent his childhood and youth until he was fully nineteen years old, and, according to Schoening's expression, made special use of the desirable opportunity he had here to gather knowledge, as well as to develop the splendid spiritual gifts with which nature had equipped him; He also made himself well acquainted with the oldest pagan Skalden poems, which had been diligently collected by Sämund Frode, as well as with the historical works of this author, as well as with those of Are Frode and several others. According to this, Snorre, through John Loptson's instruction and splendid collection of books, laid the first foundation for the taste and scholarship that have made his name immortal.

Sturleson, Snorre (Translation to German Mohnike, Gottlieb): Heimskringla - Sagen der Könige Norwegens, Stralsund 1837, pp. 315-316.

AA "[...] On the advice and with the support of his brother Thord Sturleson, Snorre married Herdise, a daughter of the rich priest Berse, who lived at **Borg** in Myre Syssel, when he was 21 years old. [...]"

Sturleson, Snorre (Translation to Norwegian Aall, Jacob): Norske Kongers Sagaer, Christiania 1838, p. II.

BB **Jarl**. This high office, the most important in the kingdom next to that of the king, for which there was no equivalent in Sweden after its abolition, is quite old, although it is not possible to say with certainty when it was introduced. In the earliest times there were several jarls at the same time in different provinces; only later were the offices united in one hand, when the holder of the office called himself "Svears and Göthers Jarl." The first to be mentioned in the council list was Ottar, Jarl at Erik Segersäll, and a total of 27 such are mentioned.

It is nevertheless probable that in certain provinces several held the office, and some were also invested with the title, for the nearest relatives of the jarl were called "jarlborn," and more than one bore this appellation, to which, however, no power was attached. Birger Jarl to Bjälbo is properly the last Jarl; but his son Magnus and his brother Erik were made Dukes: with the title the Jarlship was considered equivalent, while in Latin the word is translated as Dux, which gave it a place among the Jarls of the kingdom. The office was revived in the person of Bengt Algotsson by Magnus Smek; but ended with his death forever.

As the whole martial and judicial power was united in this official, and as he might be regarded as the alter ego of the king, and as even certain provinces were subordinated to him as liable to taxation, the office might become quite malignant in the hands of an arrogant or less well-meaning person, and was therefore justly abolished as soon as the state system had become more orderly. At his inauguration it was so done that the whole court was summoned by trumpet blasts; and when the king ascended his throne, the jarl sat down on its steps. Then the king rose, made a short address to the jarl, presented him with a sword as a token of his dignity, took him by the hand, and led him to the place of honor intended for him.

Berg, Per Gustaf: Art. Jarl, in: Svenskt Konversations – Lexikon, Second Part, Stockholm 1847, pp. 265-266.

CC Galin, Håkan, son of the Lagman of Wermland [Värmland] Folkvider, a respected and powerful man, was close to being elected King of Norway in 1204, succeeding Håkan; which, however, was prevented by the fact that he was not born a Norwegian, but a Swede. Instead, Inge Bardson, his half-brother and King Sverre's nephew, was elected king, whereupon the government was entrusted to Håkan Galin, who was therefore entitled Imperial Governor, Count or Jarl of Norway. He married in the same year Christina, the granddaughter of Erik the Saint.

Berg, Per Gustaf: Art. Galin, in: Svenskt Konversations – Lexikon, First Part, Stockholm 1845, p. 606.

DD   SKULE BÅRDSSON, norrön [Old (West) Norse] Skúli Bárðarson, **Skule Jarl**, Duke Skule, born 1189, died 24 may 1240.

Skule Bårdsson was a Norwegian Jarl, later Duke and heir to the throne. He was the son of Bård Guttormsson on Rein and half-brother of King Inge Bårdsson. Skule was imperial administrator for his son-in-law, King Håkon Håkonsson. As Håkon gained power, Skule's power was reduced, and he eventually rebelled openly against his son-in-law. Skule had himself proclaimed king of Norway in 1239. The following year he was killed by Håkon's men.

"Skule Bårdsson". Store norske leksikon, Per Norseng, 8. mai 2018, https://snl.no/Skule_Bårdsson. Accessed 13 June 2021.

EE   Håkon IV. **Håkonsson**, Håkon the Old, born after the death of his father in 1204 at Folkenborg (Folkisberg) in present-day Eidsberg, Østfold, died December 15, 16, or 17, 1263 at Kirkwall in Orkney, was king of Norway between 1217 and 1263. He was the son of King Håkon III. Sverresson of Norway (1177-1204) and his wife Inga of Varteig (c. 1185-1234). Håkon Håkonsson also became king of Iceland and Greenland.

„Håkon Håkonsson". Wikipedia.se, 27 augusti 2020, https://sv.wikipedia.org/wiki/Håkon Håkonsson. Accessed 14 June 2021.

FF   Gestilren is the name of a plain stretching between Dala and Kongslena in western Gothland. This place has become known in Swedish history through the famous battle that took place here in 1210 between the Swedish kings Sverker the Younger and Erik Knutsson, in which the former, at the head of a Danish army, tried to reconquer his kingdom, which Erik had taken possession of. The Danes were badly beaten, and King Sverker himself fell, it is said, at the hands of his own son-in-law, the powerful Folkung Sune. Many Folkungers fell in the same battle, without it being possible to say with certainty whether they fought for or against King Sverker. At Gestilren, several old monuments still remind us of this battle, such as the King's Bridge, where King Sverker fell, and the King's Hill, from which the Danish king is said to have observed the battle. Numerous finds of weapons from that time have also been made at this place.

Berg, Per Gustaf: Art. Gestilren, in: Svenskt Konversations – Lexikon, First Part, Stockholm 1845, pp. 629-630.

GG   Länsman was in earlier times a title which brought with it greater prestige and power than in our days. It is true that Sweden had no feudal system, like the feudal constitution in southern and western Europe; but the right of the king to grant fiefs was nevertheless an ancient right of the regent of the Swedish people, and he who held a fief of the king was called the king's liegeman [länsman] or also liege lord. The fiefs were not hereditary, and the possession of these lands actually included the right to collect the crown's revenues from certain estates and places. Sometimes old documents speak of "læn opa räkenskap" ["fiefs on account", ed.], i.e. fiefs in which the feudal lord was a kind of governor who collected the crown's taxes. Fiefs of the crown's own estates also occurred. Often the feudal lord was a court official by the king's grace in the countryside, and the fief made up the salary. [...]

Berg, Per Gustaf: Art. Länsman, in: Svenskt Konversations – Lexikon, Second Part, Stockholm 1847, p. 717.

Carl Johan "Janne" Jakob Keyser, born on 5 July 1821 in the parish of Slaka, Östergötland Län, died on 7 April 1895 in Norrköping, was a Swedish agricultural scientist and lecturer. Keyser entered Uppsala University in 1841 and graduated with a Master's degree in philosophy in 1848, after which he was called back to Uppsala University as a lecturer in agricultural chemistry.

In 1853-54 he undertook a scientific journey through Germany and France on a scholarship and later became a teacher at the technical school in Norrköping. In 1877-88 he was a lecturer at the same school. Keyser published a number of scientific papers.

The family roots of the translator and editor **Albert George Viktorsson Trolle** lie within sight of the fabled Yew Island (Taxus baccata), where Wieland is said to have kept a smithy. These roots, in the long-disputed border region between Denmark and Sweden, have contributed to his enthusiasm for historical subjects since early childhood.

Today he lives with his wife and children on the southernmost edge of historic Iarnwith.

This book is also available in German:

Carl Joh. Jac. Keyser

mit großem Glossar

Über die Isländische Republik
und ihren Untergang

Hrsg. Albert George Viktorsson Trolle